The Ultimate Mickey Mantle Trivia Book

The Ultimate Mickey Mantle Trivia Book
A Citadel Quiz Book

★

Tom Burkard

A Citadel Press Book
Published by Carol Publishing Group

Copyright © 1997 Tom Burkard

All rights reserved. No part of this book may be reproduced in any form, except by a newspaper or magazine reviewer who wishes to quote brief passages in connection with a review.

A Citadel Press Book
Published by Carol Publishing Group
Citadel Press is a registered trademark of Carol Communications, Inc.

Editorial, sales and distribution, and rights and permissions inquiries should be addressed to Carol Publishing Group, 120 Enterprise Avenue, Secaucus, N.J. 07094.

In Canada: Canadian Manda Group, One Atlantic Avenue, Suite 105, Toronto, Ontario M6K 3E7

Carol Publishing Group books may be purchased in bulk at special discounts for sales promotion, fund-raising, or educational purposes. Special editions can be created to specifications. For details, contact Special Sales Department, Carol Publishing Group, 120 Enterprise Avenue, Secaucus, N.J. 07094.

Designed by Andrew B. Gardner

Manufactured in the United States of America

10 9 8 7 6 5 4 3 2 1

Library of Congress Cataloging-in-Publication Data

Burkard, Tom.
    The ultimate Mickey Mantle trivia book / by Tom Burkard.
       p. cm.
    "A Citadel Press Book."
    ISBN 0-8065-1893-6 (pb)
      1. Mantle, Mickey, 1931-1995 —Miscellaneous. 2. Baseball players—United States—Biography. 3. New York Yankees (Baseball team—History). I. Title.
  GV865.M33B87   1997
  796.357'092—dc21
  [B]   97-12712
                                                                CIP

In loving memory of my mother, Victoria V. Lytkowski Burkard (December 2, 1906–February 9, 1996). She was my greatest influence and inspiration in life. Always patient, encouraging, supportive, and loving to me through many experiences and ventures, she was always there when I needed someone to talk to. Mom is missed tremendously, but remembered every day in prayer and thoughts.

Contents

Introduction	ix
Mickey Mantle Trivia Questions	**1**
True or False	3
Multiple Choice	13
Fill in the Blank	81
Mickey Remembered	89
Acknowledgments	97
Mickey Mantle Trivia Answers	**99**

Introduction

Mickey Mantle both inspired and influenced me as a young man. Back in 1960, on my first organized baseball team in the South Amboy, N.J., Midget League, Coach McCoy and Coach Skarzynski asked me what position I would like to play. I told them, "Center field, just like Mickey," and that was where I played for a couple of games until taking over as catcher. I also wore number 7 exclusively from 1961 to 1966 in the South Amboy Little Fellas League, and in the Babe Ruth League, but it wasn't always easy to get that coveted number. The older and bigger guys usually grabbed any uniform they preferred, and of course someone always wanted the Mick's number—but none as badly as I did. When uniforms were distributed at a few of our spring trainings, I had a real dogfight on my hands to acquire my idol's number, and can remember begging and pleading with our team's seasoned veterans to let me have my treasured number 7.

As a Babe Ruth League rookie in 1964, the late and great Billy Clayton (who had the ability to become a pro baseball player), had dibs on 7, so to get it for myself I had to do a lot of bribing, such as promising to shine his spikes and to bring him free Juicy Fruit gum before each game. I also wore number 7 throughout most of my twenty-year softball career, and much of my sixteen years in amateur basketball.

I saw the Yankees at the Stadium for the first time in my life in 1961, and ended up going to about three or four games that year. It was a phenomenal year for the Yankees, and especially for Mickey Mantle and Roger Maris, who were chasing Babe Ruth's home-run record. Ten years old at the time, I was lucky enough to see them blast several homers at the ballpark, and countless round-trippers on our old black-and-white television. "Ballantine blasts," as Mel Allen referred to home runs, were a common occurrence for the New York Yankees of that era.

In 1962, a group of our neighborhood friends went to see the movie *Safe at Home,* which featured the M&M Boys, better known as Mickey Mantle and Roger Maris. It was an excellent film, and I looked for a copy of it for many years, until recently acquiring one for my own Mickey Mantle collection. I still get a kick out of watching Mickey and Roger playing in their prime. It seems as though it was a lifetime ago—perhaps a better lifetime.

As teenagers, my friends and I took the subway to Yankee Stadium to a game one afternoon and got there early in hopes of getting players' autographs. In my case there was only one that mattered. Our group hung out by the players' old parking lot near the players' entrance to the Stadium, and I bagged plenty of autographs but couldn't get close to Mantle, who was mobbed by a huge throng of youngsters and signed only one autograph that day.

To return to my younger days, I can recall writing my first book report at St. Mary's Grammar School on *Mickey Mantle: The Indispensable Yankee,* by Dick Schaap. Since then, I have read almost every book ever written about Mickey, and my undying interest in him has led me to write this book.

In the early 1960s I watched the night game on WPIX when Mickey's leg gave out and he collapsed while he was running down to first base. Millions of Mantle fans—myself included—were horrified by this injury to our superhero. About a month later, on a family swimming trip to Thompson Park in Jamesburg, New Jersey, I begged my sister to put the Yankees game on the radio. Mickey pinch-hit for the first

Introduction

time since the injury, and hit a dramatic game-winning homer. I screamed with joy—the Mick was back! The Yankees would surely win the pennant!

When Mickey Mantle Day was held at the Stadium on June 8, 1969, I couldn't make it, due to a more important date. It was the day of my graduation from St. Mary's High School, in South Amboy, and the fabulous Class of '69 was marching down the aisle to "Pomp and Circumstance" on that same memorable Sunday.

My long-awaited chance to meet Mickey Mantle didn't arrive until 1978, when my best friend, Al Gomolka Jr., invited me to go to a baseball card show at Hofstra University. When Al told me that Mickey would be signing autographs there, he didn't have to ask twice. We rounded up our old buddy, Frank Jonason, and headed off to the show. Joe Pepitone was also signing, but the line for Mickey was huge. We had to wait for about an hour in the scorching gym, which had no air conditioning, but it was well worth it.

The opportunity I had lived for, the dream I had always envisioned, was almost reality. I nervously tried to think of what to say as I went up to the signing table. Mickey's friendly smile relaxed me a bit, but as I handed him my scrapbook (which I'd hurriedly thrown together earlier in the week), I somehow managed to blurt out something like "Hello Mick, you were always my favorite player. You're the greatest." He took the scrapbook, glanced through it, said it was "really nice," and asked if I had made it. He then wanted to know how to sign it, and even personalized it, writing: "To Tom, Best Wishes, Mickey Mantle."

This show was the first of hundreds that Mantle would do through the years. I still have the autograph, although the scrapbook fell apart, and I have since made a new one, over five hundred pages long. The autograph is one of my most prized possessions, as is the picture Al Gomolka Jr. took of me standing by the autograph table, looking on as Mickey signed my scrapbook. I've had the photo enlarged and framed.

Was I obsessed with Mickey? Yes, but I was far from alone, as you readers can attest. Millions of youngsters in the 1950s and '60s wanted to grow up to be a ballplayer just like him. How many of you have ever tried switch-hitting? Or emulated the way he ran the bases after hitting a home run, with his head down? Wore number 7, or had to fight for it as I did?

When we were kids back in the 1950s and '60s, we had no idea of the ill effects of alcohol or drugs. We certainly never thought that our idol had a drinking problem. On the field, he was our baseball god, and could do no wrong. Only those close to him knew of his problem, and most of them were drinking almost as much as he was. No one tried to help him overcome his demons, but back then, how many drug and alcohol rehabs or Betty Ford Centers were there? To party hearty was an accepted way of life during his playing days, and a macho thing for most ballplayers to celebrate their victories and forget their defeats at the bar after a game. If the Mick were playing today, he would be under the news media's microscope; the world would know of his problem, and he would be treated.

It was extremely sad for Mickey's millions of fans to see him suffering in the last couple of months of his life, but here was a guy who always felt that he would die at forty, as his father and grandfather had, and he survived until sixty-three. He cleaned up his entire act—as husband and father—but unfortunately too late. His plea for organ donors, however, has been a great help to our society.

Mickey Mantle was, is, and always will be my favorite baseball player, and if I'm ever invited to play in an Old-Timers softball game, you can rest assured that I will be wearing number 7 in honor of Mickey Mantle. God bless ya', Mick, and thanks for so many wonderful memories.

And I hope you, the reader, will enjoy searching your memory banks for answers to the intriguing questions on the following pages.

The Ultimate Mickey Mantle Trivia Book

The Mick takes an awesome cut in batting practice at Yankee Stadium in 1967.

Mickey Mantle Trivia Questions

True or False

Mickey Mantle had all the tools necessary to be a bona fide superstar—lightning-like speed, quite possibly the most natural power of any player in history, and he was blessed with a strong throwing arm. He could also hit for a high batting average, as is attested by his .353, which won the batting crown in 1956, and he finished second in 1957 with a blistering .365 mark. Stars of the 1990s, such as Tony Gwynn, Wade Boggs, Paul Molitor, Chuck Knoblauch, and young phenom Alex Rodriguez, have been batting champions or consistent challengers for the title almost every year. All of these modern ballplayers would qualify for the "Mickey Mantle Elite Batting Champions Club."

Hit safely on 70 of the 109 true-or-false questions and you become an official member of the "Mickey Mantle Elite Batting Champions Club."

Answer 55 to 69 questions correctly and you're in the .285 to .290 range.

Good Luck!

True or False

1. Mickey's middle name was Charles.
2. When Mickey was a youngster, his family moved to Irving, Texas.
3. In the summer of 1948, Mantle played for the Baxter Springs Whiz Kids.
4. The first professional team Mick played on in the minor leagues was the Topeka Outlaws.
5. After the conclusion of his first minor league season, Mantle worked at the post office.
6. Marian was Mickey's wife.
7. He topped the Class C League in 1950 with 141 runs scored.
8. Mickey was called up by the Yankees at the end of the 1950 season.
9. In 1951, approximately 750 people lived in the Mick's hometown of Commerce, Oklahoma.
10. Mickey's father died in 1954.
11. The Mick belted 23 home runs in 1952.
12. He hit the longest home run in history, in 1953, at Griffith Stadium. The ball went out of the stadium and was measured at 600 feet.

True or False

13. Mantle won his second successive M.V.P. Award in 1957.
14. He won his last M.V.P. Award in 1966.
15. Mickey stroked 3,002 hits in his career.
16. The Mick topped the majors with 59 four-baggers in 1956.
17. Mickey and his wife were married in 1951.
18. He signed with the Yankees in 1949 for $550.
19. Mickey's 145 RBIs led the American League in 1956.
20. He blasted his four hundredth career homer in 1962.
21. In 1956, he was the American League MVP, the Sporting News Player of the Year, and winner of the Hitchcock Belt.
22. Mantle and Maris combined for a record 115 dingers in 1961.
23. Mick blasted 7 pinch-hit home runs in his career.
24. Mantle crashed two or more homers in one game 51 times in his career.
25. He blasted home run number 100 in 1955.

Did You Know?

Mickey started the 1951 season with the Yankees but slumped and was sent to their Kansas City farm team. Bet you didn't know that Kansas City's nickname was "Blues." Mantle did not wear uniform number 7 with the Blues. He wore number 20.

Do You Remember?

Mantle's very interesting 1986 interview on *Greats of The Game* was conducted by none other than former St. Louis Cardinals catching great and current baseball announcer Tim McCarver. Mickey played against Tim in his last World Series in 1964.

26. Mickey's high school team was nicknamed the Rattlers.

27. He holds the World Series record for runs scored with 62.

28. Mantle smashed his two-hundredth career homer in 1957.

29. The Yankees paid Mickey $50,000 in 1961

30. His 59 walks are a World Series record.

31. Mickey did not have a son named Tommy.

32. Five players reached the 500-homer plateau before the Mick did.

33. Mantle participated in 20 All-Star Games.

34. He wrote *The Quality of Courage* in 1964.

True or False

35. Bob Smith helped Mickey write *Mickey Mantle: The Education of a Baseball Player.*

36. The Mick unleashed career home run number 300 in 1961.

37. Mickey went 5 for 5 in one game only once in his career.

38. He never hit a homer in the All-Star classic.

39. Mickey's sister's name is Belinda.

40. Johnny Keane never managed Mantle.

41. The Mick orbited 410 career home runs batting left-handed.

42. He hit 164 homers batting righty.

43. Mantle reached the 400 home-run plateau in 1962.

44. Mickey earned a paltry $21,500 from the Yanks in 1956.

45. In the 1961 World Series against Cincinnati, he drilled 20 hits.

46. Mantle collected his two-thousandth hit in 1966.

47. Mick scored 2,141 runs in his career.

48. Mickey's grandfather's name was Nolan.

49. The Mick joined the elite 500-homer club in 1967.

50. His Baseball Fantasy Camp was founded in 1971.

Did You Know?

Mickey said, "The biggest thing in my baseball career was going into the Hall of Fame with Whitey."

51. In 1958, Mantle commanded a $75,000 salary from the New York Yankees.
52. Mickey's father-in-law owned a lumberyard.
53. Mick and his family rented their first home in New Jersey in the summer of 1951.
54. The Mantles never rented a New Jersey home in South Amboy.
55. One of Mickey's nicknames was the Oklahoma Legend.
56. He crunched 266 career homers at Yankee Stadium.
57. The Mick returned to the Yankees in 1970 as an announcer.
58. Mantle notched 25 career pinch hits.
59. As a rookie in 1951 he was paid $5,000.
60. Prior to the 1957 Copacabana incident, Mickey and Merlyn had dinner with his teammates and their wives at Toots Shor's.
61. The Mick launched his titanic 565-foot home run in 1953.
62. On the first Mickey Mantle Day, in 1965, he was given a surfboard.

Did You Know?

Mickey competed in four classic Home Run Derbies, won his first three, and earned $7,500 in prize money. The announcer for each game was Mark Scott.

True or False

63. Mantle chalked up 2,002 career walks.
64. In 1952, Mickey received $10,000 from the Yanks.
65. Mickey played shortstop for the last time in 1951.
66. His dad worked at the Sea Gull Nest mine in Oklahoma.
67. Mick's 1954 contract amounted to $15,000.
68. Playing for the Miami Whiz Kids in 1948, Mickey blasted 3 homers into a river in one game. Fans passed around a straw hat and collected $100 for him.
69. In the off-season of 1949, he worked in a mine and earned $33 a week.
70. Mantle received his first draft notice in 1949.
71. He served with the U.S. Marine Corps during the Korean War.
72. Mickey played center field in his first World Series game.
73. Mick and his family rented their last New Jersey home in Sayreville.
74. Mickey earned $72,000 from the New York Yankees in 1959.
75. He hit 18 inside-the-park home runs in his career.
76. Mantle gained election to the Hall of Fame in 1974.
77. In the Hall of Fame balloting, he received a perfect 365 votes.
78. Mickey and Bob Costas did the *500 Home-Run Club* video together.
79. In 1960 his Yankees pact was for $65,000.
80. Art Ditmar was not one of the pallbearers at the Mantle funeral.

81. The Mick's first big league home run came in 1951 and traveled 511 feet.

82. In 1956, he became the second player in history to hit a home run over the roof of Briggs Stadium.

83. Mickey hit back-to-back homers 10 times in his career.

84. Mantle teamed with Phil Pepe in 1991 to write the bestseller My Favorite Summer, 1956.

85. The Oklahoma Sun covered Mickey's Baxter Springs Whiz Kids' baseball games.

86. Mick graduated from high school in 1949.

87. A deranged Red Sox fan threatened to shoot Mickey in 1953.

88. In 1967 Mickey wrote *My Life As a Yankee*.

89. *The Mick* was a 1985 bestseller written by Mantle and Herb Gluck.

90. Mickey's final home run, number 536, was hit at Yankee Stadium on September 20, 1968.

91. The 1956 Yankees team was Mickey's all-time favorite.

92. Mick's playing weight in 1961 was 200 pounds.

93. After skipping out early on the Yankees' postseason trip to Japan in 1955, he was fined $500.

Do You Remember?

The Mick did a television commercial for Edwards and Hanley Brokers during his playing career.

True or False

94. Early in his career, Mickey stayed at the Soreno Hotel in St. Petersburg, Florida.

95. Mantle once said that Ralph Houk was "almost like a father to me."

96. When he retired, he was using a 30-ounce baseball bat.

97. On his 1951 Bowman rookie card, Mickey's weight is listed at 175 pounds.

98. Mickey's last Topps baseball card was in 1968.

99. Mantle's last cover picture and feature story in *Baseball Digest* was in the February 1969 issue.

100. Mickey hit safely in 10 consecutive All-Star Games, to share the record.

101. At a three-hour sports memorabilia show, he could sign 500 autographs.

102. As a rookie, Mickey unknowingly gave a phony agent 50 percent of his salary.

103. The most doubles Mantle hit in one season were 37, in 1968.

104. Mickey's 1955 salary was $10,000.

105. Mickey set a record by hitting home runs from both sides of the plate in a game 10 times.

106. His 1953 baseball contract was for $11,000.

107. Mantle holds the record for spending his entire 20-year career with one team.

108. When he batted righty, Mickey would occasionally borrow a 36-ounce bat from Joe Collins.

109. Mickey Mantle died on August 13, 1995.

Mickey pouring on the speed to first base in 1964. In his younger days, he was clocked by several scouts as the fastest runner in history going from home plate to first base.

Mickey Mantle Trivia Questions

Multiple Choice

Mickey Mantle was a true home-run champion, one of the game's greatest power hitters. Now, in the 1990s, players like Mark McGwire, Frank Thomas, Ken Griffey Jr., Brady Anderson, Albert Belle, Juan Gonzalez, Jay Buhner, Mo Vaughn, Cecil Fielder, Andres Galarraga, Bobby Bonds, Gary Sheffield, Todd Hundley, and Sammy Sosa are blasting "dingers" out of major league ballparks at record-setting paces. By hitting 40 or more homers in a season, all of the previously mentioned players would definitely make the grade and become a member of the "Mickey Mantle Elite Home-Run Hitters Club."

If you answer 170 of the 340 multiple choice questions correctly, you, too, will become a member of the "Mickey Mantle Elite Home-Run Hitters Club."

Connect on 115 to 169 answers, and you're in the 25 to 30 home runs per year category.

Give it a ride!

Multiple Choice

1. Mickey was named after

   a. Mickey Wright
   b. Mickey Owen
   c. Mickey Cochrane

2. His father's name was

   a. Alan
   b. Alvan
   c. Elvin

3. His dad's nickname was

   a. Mutt
   b. Butts
   c. Buck

4. Mickey's mother's name was

   a. Ida
   b. Rochell
   c. Lovell

5. Mickey's father worked as a

   a. lead miner
   b. barber
   c. banker

Multiple Choice

6. His twin brothers were named

    a. Roy and Ray
    b. Tom and Tim
    c. Rick and Ron

7. The high school Mantle attended was

    a. Oklahoma City
    b. Spavinaw
    c. Commerce

8. When he was kicked in the left shin at football practice in 1946, Mickey developed

    a. osteomyelitis
    b. shin splints
    c. torn cartilage

9. The high school sport Mantle did not participate in was

    a. basketball
    b. golf
    c. football

Did You Know?

Mickey Mantle's monument reads: "Mickey Mantle; A great teammate; 1931–1995; 536 home runs; Winner of Triple Crown, 1956; Most World Series Homers, 18; Selected to All-Star Game 20 times; Won MVP Award, 1956, 1957, 1962; Elected to Hall of Fame 1974; A Magnificent Yankee who left a legacy of Unequaled Courage. Dedicated by the New York Yankees, August 25, 1996."

> **Did You Know?**
>
> When Mantle officially retired on March 1, 1969, he told the press, "I just can't hit anymore, and there's no use trying."

10. During the summer of 1948, where did Mantle work?

    a. a car wash
    b. a lead mine
    c. a cemetery

11. Mickey was signed to a New York Yankees contract in 1949 by   .

    a. Joe Jaskowiak
    b. Tom Greenwade
    c. Don Green

12. Mickey's first minor league manager was

    a. Harry Craft
    b. Johnny Pesky
    c. Eddie "Buddy" Popowski

13. Where did Mickey meet his future wife?

    a. the movies
    b. a football game
    c. a diner

Multiple Choice

14. In 1950, Mick's minor league Class C contract was with

a. Toledo
b. Joplin
c. Tacoma

15. In 1950, he topped the Class C League in hits with

a. 199
b. 150
c. 205

16. He was also the Class C League batting champion in 1950 with an average of

a. .356
b. .401
c. .383

17. He reported to his first major league spring training camp in 1951 at

a. Ft. Lauderdale
b. St. Petersburg
c. Phoenix

18. In July of 1951, he hit a slump and was sent to the Triple A farm team in

a. Kansas City
b. Richmond
c. Binghampton

19. In the second game of the 1951 World Series against the New York Giants, Mickey injured his knee by

a. crashing into the wall
b. stealing second base
c. catching his foot on a drainpipe

20. The 1951 World Series injury was diagnosed as

    a. torn cartilage
    b. torn ligaments
    c. bone spurs

21. Before his game number two injury in the 1951 World Series, Mick was in right field. Patrolling center was

    a. Hank Bauer
    b. Joe DiMaggio
    c. Tom Henrich

22. Mickey's roommate in 1952 was

    a. Whitey Ford
    b. Billy Martin
    c. Yogi Berra

23. In 1952 Mantle batted

    a. .294
    b. .330
    c. .311

24. During that same season, how many runs did the Mick drive in?

    a. 95
    b. 75
    c. 87

25. Mantle's first son, born in 1953, was named

Multiple Choice

a. Mickey Jr.
b. Danny
c. Elvin

26. A special announcement made at an exhibition game in 1953 stated that

a. Mickey had been drafted by the army
b. The Korean War was over
c. Mickey had become a father

27. He won the American League batting title in 1956 with an average of?

a. .333
b. .349
c. .353

28. After his standout 1956 season his second son was born, and his name was

a. Fred
b. Philip
c. David

29. His batting average in 1957 was

a. .365
b. .330
c. .350

Did You Know?

Mickey established the Mickey Mantle Hodgkins Disease Research Foundation. The first contribution was for $10,000 from the late Cardinal Spellman of New York.

30. Mickey won the American League home-run crown in 1960 by belting

a. 37
b. 40
c. 35

31. In 1965, The Mick's average dipped to

a. .255
b. .241
c. .229

32. After a tough 1965, he managed to raise his batting average in 1966 to

a. .269
b. .301
c. .288

33. Sixty thousand fans attended the second Mickey Mantle Day at Yankee Stadium on

a. July 3, 1968
b. June 8, 1969
c. August 13, 1969

34. Inducted into the Hall of Fame on the same day as Mantle was

a. Yogi Berra
b. Duke Snider
c. Whitey Ford

35. Mantle's popular New York restaurant is called

    a. The Lucky 7
    b. Mickey Mantle's
    c. Yankee Land

36. In 1952, Mickey's top challenger for Joe DiMaggio's vacated center field post was

    a. Jackie Jensen
    b. Allie Clark
    c. Gene Woodling

Did You Know?

The Mickey Mantle monument at Yankee Stadium is 5 feet high, 3 feet wide, and 1 foot deep. It weighs 3,000 pounds, and its base adds another 1,500 pounds.

---

37. The number of world champion clubs Mantle played for was

    a. 2
    b. 7
    c. 10

38. Before his death in 1995, Mickey established

    a. Mickey Mantle Donor Awareness Foundation
    b. Mickey Mantle Cancer Aid
    c. Mickey Mantle Organization for Transplants

39. Mick's mother's maiden name was

    a. Smith
    b. Richardson
    c. Kurtz

40. In 1968, his final year, his contract called for

   a. $100,000
   b. $75,000
   c. $1,000,000

41. Mickey's popular restaurant in New York City is located at

   a. at 42 Central Park South
   b. on 45th Street
   c. on the West Side

42. He received a proclamation from the City of New York designating September 18 Mickey Mantle Day in

   a. 1969
   b. 1960
   c. 1965

43. Not on Mantle's favorite list of hobbies was

   a. hunting
   b. tennis
   c. golf

44. In 1956 the Maryland Professional Baseball Association awarded him the

   a. Maryland Champion of the Year
   b. Babe Ruth Sultan of Swat
   c. Most Courageous Athlete

45. The Mick was a boyhood idol of

Multiple Choice

   a. Tony Kybek
   b. Tom Tresh
   c. Phil Linz

46. Mickey was once a national spokesman for

   a. Nissan
   b. Schick
   c. Cystic Fibrosis

47. He appeared in more games than any other Yankee in history. He played in

   a. 2,401
   b. 2,142
   c. 2,039

48. Mantle's career home-run ratio was

   a. 12.3
   b. 15.12
   c. 10.4

49. In 1962, the Mick received the Most Courageous Athlete Award from

   a. New York Baseball Writers
   b. National Baseball Writers
   c. Philadelphia Sportswriters

50. In 1952, he was selected Oklahoma Athlete of the Year and received the

   a. Griggs Trophy
   b. John Mobley Award
   c. Mayor John T. O'Leary Award

51. Mantle holds the all-time World Series home-run record by hitting

   a. 21
   b. 17
   c. 18

52. He rocketed his first career homer out of

   a. Shibe Park
   b. Memorial Stadium
   c. Comiskey Park

53. Mantle's career batting average was

   a. .300
   b. .304
   c. .298

54. Mickey holds the World Series mark for RBIs with

   a. 54
   b. 48
   c. 40

55. The number of home-run crowns in Mantle's possession is

   a. 6
   b. 7
   c. 4

56. The song from the 1950s written about Mantle was?

   a. "He's a Star"
   b. "I Love Mickey"
   c. "Number 7 Is My Man"

57. The song was performed by Mickey (who had a few words), and by

   a. Theresa Brewer
   b. Doris Day
   c. Beverly Kovacs

58. The Mantles *did not* have a son named

   a. Danny
   b. Tim
   c. Billy

Did You Know?

Rawlings produced special game balls for the Yankees-Athletics contest that was played at Yankee Stadium on the day of the dedication of the Mickey Mantle monument at Yankee Stadium, August 25, 1996. Each baseball had number 7 imprinted on it.

---

59. In 1946 he played in an amateur league for teenagers called the Ban Johnson League, and his team was the

   a. Commerce, Oklahoma
   b. Miami, Oklahoma
   c. Spavinaw Oklahoma

60. In his first minor league season as a shortstop at Independence, the number of errors Mantle committed was

   a. 3
   b. 27
   c. 47

61. The Yankee veteran who bought Mickey a new glove during his first spring training in 1950 was

   a. Ralph Houk
   b. Frank Crosetti
   c. Eddie Lopat

62. In the spring of 1951, Mantle's coach on the art of playing the outfield was

a. Johnny Lindell
b. Tommy Henrich
c. George Selkirk

63. How many times did Mickey lead the American League in slugging percentage?

a. 2
b. 3
c. 7

Did You Know?

In the movie *City Slickers*, actor Billy Crystal said that his greatest day was the first time his dad took him to Yankee Stadium, where he saw Mantle play.

64. He ripped his first big league hit off of

a. Mel Parnell
b. Bill Wight
c. Bob Feller

65. His two roommates as a rookie in 1951 were

Multiple Choice

a. Johnny Hopp and Hank Bauer
b. Yogi Berra and Phil Rizzuto
c. Eddie Lopat and Johnny Sain

66. Al Silverman's book about Mickey was titled

a. *Mickey Mantle: Mr. Yankee*
b. *The Commerce Kid*
c. *The Life and Times of Mickey Mantle*

67. Rooming with Mickey in New York during the 1961 season were

a. Roger Maris and Bob Cerv
b. Whitey Ford and Clete Boyer
c. Joe Pepitone and Tom Tresh

68. Mickey, Whitey Ford, and their wives met which famous actress in 1961?

a. Marilyn Monroe
b. Betty Grable
c. Jayne Mansfield

69. In 1988, he did a public service advertisement for

a. The Blindness Foundation
b. American Cancer Society
c. Deafness Research Foundation

70. In all of his business ventures, Mickey never owned?

a. oil wells
b. a bowling center
c. a record company

71. How many times did he lead the American League in runs scored?

a. 6
b. 9
c. 4

72. 1967 marked the fifth consecutive year that Mickey's contract called for

a. $100,000
b. $120,000
c. $85,000

73. During the later stages of his career, Mantle had late-inning replacements in center field (caddies) in order to gain rest for his legs. A Yankee who did not caddy for him was

a. Jack Reed
b. Bobby Bonds
c. Ross Moschitto

74. In 1967, Mickey Mantle played in his 2,165th game as a Yankee to set a new team record, passing

a. Babe Ruth
b. Joe DiMaggio
c. Lou Gehrig

75. The May 30, 1968, Memorial Day doubleheader at Yankee Stadium against the Senators marked the Mick's last great game, when he

a. hit 3 homers and drove in 7 runs
b. went 5 for 5, with 2 home runs and 5 RBIs
c. had 4 hits, including a grand slam and 6 runs batted in

Do You Remember?

Mantle defeated Ernie Banks 5–3 in an exciting Home-Run Derby Contest.

Multiple Choice

76. His 535th homer moved him on the all-time home-run list ahead of

   a. Ted Williams
   b. Ralph Kiner
   c. Jimmy Foxx

77. Mantle and Whitey Ford once did a commercial for

   a. Right Guard
   b. Carvel ice cream
   c. Chevrolet

78. As a youngster, he moved up from playing in the Pee Wee League to the

   a. Babe Ruth League
   b. Gabby Street League
   c. Junior League

79. Mickey received his high school diploma during the day instead of the evening with his graduating class because

   a. his dad was ill
   b. he had a big game to play in front of a Yankee Scout
   c. he was in the hospital

80. He signed his first Yankee contract in 1949 in

   a. a car
   b. his high school coach's office
   c. his mother's kitchen

81. As a Yankee rookie, where did Mickey share an apartment with two other veterans?

   a. next to Madison Square Garden
   b. on Broadway
   c. upstairs from the Stage Deli

82. His favorite hobby off the field was

   a. hunting
   b. golf
   c. fishing

83. Mickey's roommate in 1965 was

   a. Jim Bouton
   b. Joe Pepitone
   c. Whitey Ford

> ### Did You Know?
>
> Mickey was a celebrity captain in Troy Aikman's Celebrity Golf Tournament in April 1995.

84. Mickey, Whitey Ford, and Billy Martin were sometimes called

   a. Three Brothers
   b. T.H.E. Boys
   c. Three Amigos

85. His five hundredth home run was surrendered by

   a. Hoyt Wilhem
   b. Jim Bunning
   c. Stu Miller

86. Mickey's overall batting average in All-Star Games was

    a. .273
    b. .333
    c. .233

87. For how many years did Casey Stengel manage Mickey?

    a. 10
    b. 14
    c. 7

88. What award did Mickey win in 1962?

    a. MVP
    b. Comeback Player of the Year
    c. Golden Glove

89. In 1985, he collaborated with Herb Gluck to write

    a. *The Mickey Mantle Story*
    b. *The Mick*
    c. *An American Legend*

90. Mickey's heritage was a mixture of

    a. Slovak and Swedish
    b. Irish and Polish
    c. Dutch and German

91. Every Christmas as a youngster, Mick's dad would buy him

    a. a baseball glove
    b. a baseball bat
    c. a bicycle

92. Mantle's 1957 salary swelled to

    a. $55,000
    b. $100,000
    c. $65,000

93. He was a partner in a Fantasy Baseball Camp which was called

   a. Heroes of the Game
   b. The Mickey Mantle/Whitey Ford Fantasy Baseball Camp
   c. Bronx Bombers Baseball Camp

94. Mickey's career total of doubles was

   a. 344
   b. 407
   c. 399

95. Mick's closest friend as a youngster was

   a. John Mansfield
   b. LeRoy Bennett
   c. Mike Roman

96. Early in his career Mickey endorsed

   a. Camels
   b. Winstons
   c. Pall Malls

97. His Commerce High School sports teams competed in what conference?

   a. Blue Sky
   b. Big Mountain
   c. Lucky Seven

98. He was sports editor for his high school newspaper, which was called?

   a. *Commerce Echo*
   b. *Tiger Chat*
   c. *Tiger Talk*

99. When Tom Greenwade discovered Mickey, who was he scouting?

   a. Bobby Brown
   b. Ralph Terry
   c. Billy Johnson

Do You Remember?

In the 1953 World Series against the Dodgers, Mantle blasted a grand-slam homer in game number 5 off of "Monk" Meyer. The shot landed in the left-field upper deck.

---

100. The starting third baseman on Mantle's first pro team at Independence was

   a. Lou Skizas
   b. Clete Boyer
   c. Eddie Mathews

101. When Mantle met Merlyn, she was a

   a. cheerleader
   b. majorette
   c. scorekeeper

102. Before they were married, Merlyn worked in

  a. a bank
  b. a hospital
  c. a library

103. Mick called Merlyn at her job for their first date. She worked at

  a. a soda shop
  b. a pharmacy
  c. a high school office

Did You Know?

By 1965, Mickey's legs were so bad that his pregame ritual took over an hour. He had to use the whirlpool and massage to improve circulation, and then wrap an elastic bandage from ankle to thigh.

---

104. As a nonrostered player on the Yankees at the end of the 1950 season, Mickey roomed with

  a. Bill "Moose" Skowron
  b. Billy Martin
  c. Johnny Kucks

Multiple Choice

105. In an Old Timers game at Yankee Stadium, the Mick blasted a homer off of

    a. Bob Feller
    b. Whitey Ford
    c. Juan Marichal

106. In his brilliant career, how many runs did the Mick drive in?

    a. 1,362
    b. 1,105
    c. 1,509

107. Before being sent back to the minors in 1951, Mick was reduced to sharing right field with

    a. Tommy Henrich
    b. Jackie Jensen
    c. Johnny Mize

108. Cartoons came out in the New York newspapers in the 1950s, calling Mickey, Whitey, and Billy the

    a. Dead End Kids
    b. Party Boys
    c. Wild Bunch

109. What did Mickey contribute offensively to Don Larsen's perfect game in the 1956 World Series?

    a. 2 doubles
    b. 3 for 4
    c. a solo home run

110. Where were Mickey and Merlyn married?

    a. in New York
    b. on a train
    c. at Merlyn's parents' home

111. In 1952, the city of Commerce held a Mickey Mantle Day. What did they give him?

   a. a key to the city
   b. a set of silverware
   c. a horse

112. As a youngster, Mickey's favorite baseball idol was

   a. Stan Musial
   b. Ted Williams
   c. Mickey Cochrane

113. Mickey's agent in 1956 was

   a. Frank Scott
   b. Steve Schmid
   c. Gene O'Toole

114. In what business venture did Mantle become involved in 1957?

   a. Mickey Mantle Barbecue Chicken
   b. Mickey Mantle Holiday Inn
   c. Mickey Mantle Bowling Alley

115. His partner for many years in the Fantasy Baseball Camp business was

   a. Whitey Ford
   b. Yogi Berra
   c. Billy Martin

Multiple Choice

116. Mantle's lawyer for many years was

   a. Roy True
   b. Stan Grzes
   c. Ron Poulsen

117. Who was *not* involved in the famous Copacabana brawl in 1957?

   a. Mickey Mantle
   b. Hank Bauer
   c. Elston Howard

118. The star entertainer at the nightclub that evening was

   a. Sammy Davis Jr.
   b. Frank Sinatra
   c. Judy Garland

119. In 1958, the Mick was called to testify before the U.S. Senate. The hearings were called

   a. Kefauver
   b. Sports and Gambling
   c. Chapin

120. The other Yankee called to testify with Mick was

   a. Casey Stengel
   b. Gil McDougald
   c. Andy Carey

Did You Know?

The final honor of Mantle's monument-dedication day went to Mickey's wonderful friend and fellow Hall of Famer Whitey Ford, who unveiled the monument.

121. How much were Mantle and Maris paid to play in the movie *Safe at Home?*

   a. $10,000
   b. $15,000
   c. $25,000

122. Mick tied Babe Ruth's World Series home-run record by hitting number 15 in 1963 against the Dodgers. The pitcher was

   a. Don Drysdale
   b. Sandy Koufax
   c. Johnny Podres

123. Toward the end of Mickey's career, the player expected by writers to be the "second Mickey Mantle" was

   a. Roger Repoz
   b. Tom Tresh
   c. Bobby Murcer

124. The country club Mantle joined in 1965 was

   a. Preston Trails
   b. Beaver Falls
   c. Fox and Quail

Do You Remember?

In game number 3 of the 1951 World Series against the New York Giants, Mantle batted first, Bauer second, and Phil Rizzuto third. Mantle and Rizzuto both bunted for base hits in the first inning.

Multiple Choice

125. As of 1985, his golf handicap was

    a. 16
    b. 8
    c. 12

126. As a sportscaster on television, Mickey initially covered

    a. Olympics
    b. All-Star Game
    c. Little League World Series

127. In 1968 Mickey invested in

    a. Dial M
    b. Mickey Mantle Country Cookin'
    c. Main Man-tles

128. In 1956, the company set up for Mantle was

    a. Mickey's Men
    b. Big 7
    c. Mickey Mantle Enterprises

129. In 1973 he began public relations work for

    a. Mutual of Omaha
    b. Prudential
    c. Reserve Life Insurance

130. His one-year contract for the Claridge casino amounted to

    a. $1 million
    b. $100,000
    c. $250,000

131. Following his retirement, his function in spring training was

    a. batting instructor
    b. PR man
    c. outfield instructor

Do You Remember?

On Mickey Mantle Day on June 8, 1969, at Yankee Stadium, Mickey and Joe DiMaggio both had their plaques mounted at the ballpark.

132. The pancake mix Mick endorsed in 1956 was

   a. Aunt Jemima's
   b. Batter Up
   c. Pillsbury

133. How many career strikeouts did Mickey rack up?

   a. 1,923
   b. 1,710
   c. 1,401

134. In 1968, Mickey's Texas license plate number was

   a. 777
   b. MIC
   c. MM-7

135. The name of the public television videography that later became a tape and also a book about Mickey was

   a. *The American Dream Comes to Life*
   b. *Baseball Hero*
   c. *Mantle: The Real Legend*

136. He was never drafted into the military because of

   a. nearsightedness
   b. osteomyelitis
   c. flat feet

137. The player not questioned with Mickey by the Senate committee in Washington was

   a. Jimmy Piersall
   b. Stan Musial
   c. Ted Williams

138. For many years, Mickey and Whitey called each other what nickname

   a. Pard
   b. Boss
   c. Slick

139. The man who created the tape-measure homer by measuring Mantle's blast at Griffith Stadium was

   a. Red Foley
   b. Paul Muller
   c. Red Patterson

140. The pitcher who served up Mickey's 565-foot tape-measure homer in 1953 was

   a. Chuck Stobbs
   b. Camilio Pascual
   c. Pedro Ramos

141. During a 1951 exhibition game he blasted a homer believed to travel 600 feet, and it was hit at

   a. Miami University
   b. the Polo Grounds
   c. USC

142. In 1961 several Yankees and Mickey were guests on

  a. *The Match Game*
  b. *Password*
  c. *To Tell the Truth*

143. In 1961, Mantle's roommate on the road was

  a. Joe DeMaestri
  b. Joe Pepitone
  c. Roger Maris

144. In 1970, he worked as an announcer of

  a. *The Saturday Game of the Week*
  b. *Sports Extra*
  c. *This Week in Baseball*

145. Mickey was the first player to receive

  a. Comeback Player of the Year
  b. Hutchinson Award
  c. Babe Ruth Award

146. Attending Mickey Mantle Day in 1965 was

  a. Sen. Edward "Ted" Kennedy
  b. Robert F. Kennedy
  c. Frank Sinatra

Did You Know?

In 1968, Mantle was moved to the third spot in the batting order by Ralph Houk so he might get some better pitches to hit. Youngster Roy White moved to cleanup.

147. When the Mick retired after the 1968 season, he set a record for most home runs by a player in his final season. He hit

    a. 18
    b. 20
    c. 21

148. He holds the record for most extra-inning home runs with?

    a. 9
    b. 12
    c. 14

149. How many times did Mickey have the most combined hits and walks?

    a. 1
    b. 2
    c. 5

150. Who was the pitcher he victimized for 13 career home runs?

    a. Billy Pierce
    b. Early Wynn
    c. Bill Tarallo

151. In 1964 Mickey and his son did an ad for *Look* and *Post* magazines. The company advertized was

    a. Phillies Cigars
    b. Coca Cola
    c. Kool Aid

152. The ad offered

    a. an autographed picture
    b. a Yankee baseball glove
    c. a Mickey Mantle baseball glove

153. When batting lefty, he occasionally used to borrow the 32-ounce bat of

  a. Hank Bauer
  b. Jerry Coleman
  c. Johnny Mize

154. The road leading into and out of Commerce, Oklahoma, is

  a. Mickey Mantle Boulevard
  b. Main Street
  c. Mickey Mantle Way

155. The Mantle home in Commerce is located at

  a. 7 Whippoorwill Drive
  b. 321 Main Street
  c. 319 N. Quincy

156. In 1944, Mickey played for the Gabby St. League (ages 12 to 15) champions. The team was from

  a. Douthat
  b. Commerce
  c. Picher

157. During the summer of 1947, Mantle worked

  a. for a plumber
  b. at a cemetery
  c. as a truck driver

158. In 1947 Mickey's dad owned

  a. a LaSalle
  b. a DeSoto
  c. a Ford

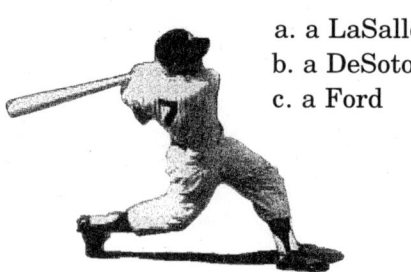

159. Playing for the Miami Whiz Kids in 1948, Mick hit 3 homers in one game, and fans collected money for him. As a result, Mantle

    a. forfeited his amateur status
    b. was arrested
    c. was suspended from school

160. Mickey's first love in 1949 was

    a. Mary Lynn Peters
    b. Lucy Gianni
    c. Jeanette Holmes

Did You Know?

Mickey Mantle and Manager Johnny Keane feuded throughout the 1965 season. Mick once said that he would have retired after the 1965 campaign if he'd been better off financially.

161. Mickey attended his senior prom with

    a. Mary Sue
    b. Merlyn
    c. Jeanette

162. How many grand slam homers did the Mick belt in his career?

    a. 9
    b. 10
    c. 14

163. One of Mickey's three roommates while playing for Independence and Joplin was

   a. Steve Kraly
   b. Ken Benson
   c. Robert Kovacs

164. Mickey's favorite song during his first minor league season was

   a. "Amanda"
   b. "Long Gone Lonesome Blues"
   c. "Your Cheatin' Heart"

165. A favorite dating spot for Mickey and his friends in Oklahoma was?

   a. Pandora's Box
   b. Cactus Flower
   c. Spook Light

166. His uniform number on the Commerce High School basketball team was

   a. 7
   b. 44
   c. 21

Did You Know?

Football Hall of Famer and current announcer Frank Gifford and Mantle shared the same locker at Yankee Stadium in 1956, and both won MVP awards, Mickey in the American League, and Gifford in the NFL.

Multiple Choice

167. The boy who was not Mickey's roommate at Joplin was?

    a. Carl Lombardi
    b. Bob Weisler
    c. Vince Poulsen

168. Mantle's early roommate, Johnny Hopp, tabbed him

    a. Young Hero
    b. The Champ
    c. Superstar

169. In late 1951, Mick was recalled by the Yankees from the Kansas City farm team. At the same time, he was again called by the draft board to report to

    a. Ft. Sill, Oklahoma
    b. Ft. Dix, New Jersey
    c. Ft. Benning, Georgia

170. In order to regain his amateur status after losing it in 1948, he had to

    a. perform community service
    b. return the $54
    c. quit the Whiz Kids

171. In the second game of the 1951 Series, a player hit a fly ball to right-center field. Mickey tried to catch it and injured his knee. The player was

    a. Bobby Thompson
    b. Monte Irvin
    c. Willie Mays

172. Casey Stengel used to call Mantle

    a. Muscles
    b. Ignatz
    c. Mack

173. He became the first player in the American League to hit homers from both sides of the plate in one game. The year was

   a. 1952
   b. 1954
   c. 1955

174. In 1956, he hit 52 homers to lead the majors. The player who finished second behind Mickey Mantle was

   a. Vic Wertz
   b. Al Kaline
   c. Ted Williams

175. Mick's biggest World Series disappointment was losing

   a. in 1955 to the Dodgers
   b. in 1960 to the Pirates
   c. in 1964 to the Cardinals

176. In 1961, Mickey and Whitey lost $10,000 each in?

   a. a health and fitness center
   b. a Canadian bomb shelter business
   c. a Roller Derby team

177. His first autobiography came out in the fall of 1956. It was called

   a. *Mickey the Great*
   b. *The Mick*
   c. *The Mickey Mantle Story*

Multiple Choice

Do You Remember?

In the last few weeks of the 1964 season, rookie Roger Repoz was Mickey's late-inning defensive replacement.

178. Mickey's Dallas bowling alley was called

    a. Southern Yankee Lanes
    b. Mickey Mantle Lanes
    c. Downtown Dallas Bowling Center

179. After Billy Martin left the Yankees via the trade route, Mick's closest friend was

    a. Whitey Ford
    b. Don Larsen
    c. Yogi Berra

180. In 1969, he was partners in an employment agency with

    a. Frank Gifford
    b. Arnold Palmer
    c. Joe Namath

181. The employment agency was called

    a. Center Field
    b. Mantle Men and Namath Girls
    c. Mantle-Palmer

182. In 1964, Mickey told a teammate to play his harmonica louder on the bus, causing big trouble with the manager, Yogi Berra. The player was

    a. Hal Reniff
    b. Jesse Gonder
    c. Phil Linz

183. In 1968, with Mantle playing first base, the center fielder was

   a. Roger Repoz
   b. Steve Whitaker
   c. Joe Pepitone

184. In 1969 spring training, Mickey announced his retirement at

   a. Yankee Clipper Hotel
   b. Howard Johnson's
   c. Holiday Inn

185. In game three of the 1964 World Series, Mantle hit the gamewinning homer in the bottom of the ninth off of

   a. Bob Gibson
   b. Barney Schultz
   c. Ray Washburn

186. At his Hall of Fame induction, Mickey was introduced by

   a. Ford Frick
   b. Bowie Kuhn
   c. George Steinbrenner

187. In 1973, Mantle defeated Whitey Ford in what type of race?

   a. auto
   b. horse
   c. swimming

188. Mickey was hospitalized in June of 1978 for

   a. a bleeding ulcer
   b. a knee replacement
   c. a liver problem

189. Mickey was banned from baseball because of his Atlantic City job by

   a. Bart Giamatti
   b. Bowie Kuhn
   c. Warren Giles

190. Mantle was reinstated by

   a. Peter Ueberroth
   b. Bowie Kuhn
   c. Lee McPhail

191. In 1962, Mickey had a cameo role in the movie *That Touch of Mink*, which starred

   a. Cary Grant and Doris Day
   b. Marilyn Monroe
   c. Ava Gardner

Did You Know?

Mickey hit his last home run off of Boston's Jim Lonborg in Yankee Stadium. Ironically, his last big-league at-bat was against Lonborg at Fenway Park on September 28, 1968, and he popped out to left field. Mickey left the game, and Andy Kosco replaced him at first base.

Did You Know?

In 1967, Steve Whitaker, who was in his first year as a Yankee, was taken under Mickey's wing. They were the only two Yanks who actually lived in Manhattan, and Mantle would take the youngster everywhere with him.

192. In the 1980s, one of Mickey's favorite Dallas sports bars was

   a. Jaxx Café
   b. Lemon Tree
   c. Cactus and Cowboys

193. Mantle's favorite Italian restaurant in Dallas in the 1980s was

   a. Villa Marotta
   b. Lianna's
   c. Capriotti's

194. Mickey and football great Pat Summerall used to do their drinking at

   a. Patty O'Brien's
   b. Stan's Bar and Grill
   c. Yankee Tavern

Multiple Choice

195. Mickey's son who died of a heart attack was named

    a. Danny
    b. Mickey Jr.
    c. Billy

196. The speaker in the pulpit at Mickey's funeral was

    a. Bobby Richardson
    b. Dr. Robert Schuller
    c. Rev. Billy Graham

197. Mick's funeral was held at

    a. Holy Trinity Church of Dallas
    b. Lover's Lane United Methodist Church of Dallas
    c. First Baptist Church of Commerce, Oklahoma

198. The principal eulogy at Mantle's funeral was delivered by

    a. Mel Allen
    b. Phil Rizzuto
    c. Bob Costas

199. The song Mickey requested to be sung at his funeral was

    a. "Yesterday When I Was Young"
    b. "My Way"
    c. "Autumn of My Life"

200. The main song at the Mick's funeral was sung by

    a. Kenny Rogers
    b. Roy Clark
    c. John Cougar Mellencamp

201. The player who was *not* a pallbearer at the funeral was

    a. Joe Pepitone
    b. Bobby Murcer
    c. John Blanchard

202. Where was Mickey laid to rest?

a. St. Peter's Cemetery
b. Parkman Hillcrest Mausoleum
c. Twelve Apostles Cemetery

203. When he was in junior high, Mickey's family moved to

a. a farm
b. the suburbs
c. the mountains

204. When he was in junior high, Mickey got to school by

a. bicycle
b. bus
c. horse

205. Mickey injured his right shoulder during the 1965 off-season by

a. lifting weights
b. falling on ice
c. playing touch football

206. At Mickey Mantle Day in 1969, he told the fans that what he missed most was

a. fans
b. home runs
c. the clubhouse

207. The bestseller Mickey wrote with Mickey Herskowitz was

a. *Pennant Fever*
b. *All My Octobers*
c. *Autumn Magic*

208. In 1950, while playing for Joplin in the Western League, he committed the most errors in the league. He made

a. 32
b. 55
c. 61

209. After the 1955 World Series, Mickey and the Yankees toured

a. Japan
b. Alaska
c. Puerto Rico

210. Mickey's most valuable rookie baseball card is

a. 1951 Bowman
b. 1951 Topps
c. 1952 Topps

211. The popular broadcaster who carries a 1958 Topps All-Star Mickey Mantle baseball card in his wallet at all times is

a. Frank Gifford
b. Curt Gowdy
c. Bob Costas

Did You Know?

During Mantle's last year, the great Rocky Colavito, for many years a rival and now a Yankee teammate, was one of Mickey's confidants.

212. Yankees superscout Tom Greenwade did *not* sign which of these players?

  a. Mickey Mantle
  b. Jerry Lumpe
  c. Jim Bouton

213. One of Mickey's favorite hangouts in New York on 52nd Street was

  a. Harper's
  b. Toots Shor's
  c. Your Father's Mustache

214. In 1960, Roger Maris hit 39 homers. Mantle tallied

  a. 40
  b. 45
  c. 38

215. In 1961, with eighteen games remaining in the season, Mickey became ill and was recommended to a doctor by

  a. Ralph Houk
  b. Mel Allen
  c. Red Barber

216. After the doctor gave him a needle, Mickey's hip became infected. As a result

  a. he sat out the rest of the season
  b. he played nine games
  c. he played two more games.

Multiple Choice 57

217. How many official World Series records does Mantle hold?

    a. 5
    b. 6
    c. 9

218. He does *not* hold the World Series record for

    a. triples
    b. RBIs
    c. home runs

219. The Mick's featured on a 1958 Topps baseball card captioned "World Series Batting Foes" with

    a. Duke Snider
    b. Eddie Mathews
    c. Hank Aaron

220. He led the American League outfielders in fielding percentage

    a. once
    b. three times
    c. twice

221. In 1966 the number of homers the Mick hit in eleven days was

    a. 7
    b. 9
    c. 11

222. In 1968, he batted a career low of

    a. .237
    b. .250
    c. .231

223. Mantle missed most of the 1963 season because of

   a. torn cartilage
   b. a shoulder injury
   c. a broken foot

224. The license plate of the golf cart that drove him around Yankee Stadium during Mickey Mantle Day in 1969 was

   a. Mick
   b. MM-7
   c. 777

225. Which newly-divorced 1962 rookie did Mick let stay with him at the St. Moritz?

   a. Joe Pepitone
   b. Al Downing
   c. Rollie Sheldon

226. The 1960s teammate of Mantle's who named one of his sons after Mickey was?

   a. Pete Mikkelsen
   b. Duke Maas
   c. Tom Tresh

227. The song written by Terry Cashman as a tribute to the Mick was

   a. "Willie, Mickey, and the Duke"
   b. "Boys of Summer"
   c. "Baseball Fever"

Did You Know?

During the last few days of the Mick's final year in 1968, his Yankee teammates all wanted their photos taken with him for precious keepsakes.

228. On a 1953 Bowman baseball card group shot, the player not featured with Mickey is

   a. Hank Bauer
   b. Yogi Berra
   c. Vic Raschi

229. As a rookie, Mantle roomed briefly with

   a. Jerry Coleman
   b. Andy Carey
   c. Jerry Lumpe

230. In his prime, Mick's neck size was

   a. 16
   b. 17
   c. 18

231. What nickname did Casey Stengel give Mickey as a rookie

   a. The Phenom
   b. The Flash
   c. Star

232. Mickey's high school football coach was

   a. Jack Skutnik
   b. Ken Rogers
   c. John Lingo

233. As a Yankee rookie, writers nicknamed him

  a. The Franchise
  b. Commerce Comet
  c. Commerce Kid

234. Toward the end of his career, his late-inning replacement in center field was

  a. Ross Moschitto
  b. Elliott Maddux
  c. Bobby Bonds

235. Mickey named his son Billy after

  a. Bill Stafford
  b. Billy Gardner
  c. Billy Martin

236. In 1968, when writer Jim Ogle asked him what his biggest thrill in baseball was, Mickey said

  a. his pinch-hit home run against Baltimore
  b. his World Series homer off of Barney Schultz
  c. his first game at Yankee Stadium

237. A 1957 Topps baseball card entitled "Yankee Power Hitters" featured the Mick and

  a. Yogi Berra
  b. Joe Collins
  c. Moose Skowton

238. Which former Cleveland Indians Manager once said "Mantle has more power than Babe Ruth did."

 a. Lou Boudreau
 b. Al Lopez
 c. Bob Lemon

239. Some scouts clocked Mickey as the fastest player in history, running from home plate to first in

 a. 2.9 seconds
 b. 3.1 seconds
 c. 4.1 seconds

240. When Mickey was injured in the 1951 World Series, he was placed in the same hospital room with

 a. his brother
 b. his father
 c. the governor of New York

241. Mickey gave which of these superstars the nickname Charlie Hustle

 a. Pete Rose
 b. Reggie Jackson
 c. Mike Schmidt

242. What was Mick most notorious for?

 a. giving hot feet
 b. kicking water coolers
 c. breaking bats

243. In 1953 the FBI was summoned because a deranged fan of an opposing team threatened to harm Mickey. How?

 a. knife him
 b. shoot him
 c. poison him

244. One of Mickey's favorite night spots in Commerce was

    a. Night Owl
    b. The Cactus and Owl
    c. 400 Club

245. While Billy Martin was in the military the Mick's roommate was

    a. Jerry Coleman
    b. Enos Slaughter
    c. Phil Rizzuto

246. The Yankee pitcher who used to pick up which pitches opposing hurlers were throwing, and signal Mickey when he was batting was?

    a. Ryne Duren
    b. Bob Turley
    c. Ralph Terry

247. After the 1955 World Series, Billy Martin and Mantle went to Hawaii and tried

    a. waterskiing
    b. skydiving
    c. surfing

248. The all-time great Hall of Famer who once lectured Mickey about not striking out so much was

    a. Ty Cobb
    b. Babe Ruth
    c. Honus Wagner

249. The 1987 book dedicated to Mickey's home runs was called

    a. *Tape Measure*
    b. *Mickey Mantle's Legendary Home Runs*
    c. *Power Blasts*

250. Mickey's nickname for Vice President Spiro T. Agnew was

    a. Archie
    b. Fritz
    c. Bouser

251. Mantle started a basketball team in the 1953 offseason and called it

    a. The Mickey Mantle Southwest Chat All-Stars
    b. Yankees All-Stars
    c. Mick's Men

252. Mickey's home run number 494 put him ahead of Lou Gehrig on the all-time list. He crashed this important round-tripper off of

    a. Bruce Howard
    b. Hoyt Wilhelm
    c. Joel Horlen

253. On Mickey Mantle Day in 1969, which groundskeeper drove Mickey around the stadium in a golf cart for the last time?

    a. Little Danny
    b. Steady Eddie
    c. Big Al

254. On NBC's *Game of the Week*, Mantle did not work with

    a. Tony Kubek
    b. Curt Gowdy
    c. Harry Caray

255. In 1961, a stripper in Texas called herself

   a. Mickey
   b. Rajah
   c. Mickey Maris

256. The book John Devaney wrote about the Mick in 1969 was called

   a. *Mantle's Magic*
   b. *The Baseball Life of Mickey Mantle*
   c. *Mr. Pinstripes*

257. In 1962, on a Topps baseball card titled "Managers Dream," Mantle was pictured with

   a. Ernie Banks
   b. Willie Mays
   c. Stan Musial

258. The player who spent much of the offseason in 1953 at the Mantle home in Commerce was

   a. Bob Hale
   b. Billy Martin
   c. Deron Johnson

259. Mickey's 1961 World Series was stopped by

   a. a groin pull
   b. an abcessed hip
   c. good pitching

260. Mickey wrote a book on heroism and bravery in 1964 called

    a. *None but the Brave*
    b. *Unsung Heroes*
    c. *The Quality of Courage*

261. On a 1960 Topps baseball card entitled "Rival All-Stars," Mickey is pictured with

    a. Ken Boyer
    b. Stan Musial
    c. Tim McCarver

262. In 1961, Mickey tied for the team lead in most runs scored with

    a. Bobby Richardson
    b. Roger Maris
    c. Tony Kubek

263. Mantle's 1991 bestseller, *My Favorite Summer,1956,* was dedicated to

    a. Billy Martin
    b. Billy Mantle
    c. Merlyn Mantle

264. The Mick's greatest overall offensive season was

    a. 1957
    b. 1961
    c. 1956

265. Who fined Mantle for cutting out early on the club when it was in Japan?

    a. Ford Frick
    b. George Weiss
    c. Joe Cronin

266. In 1961 Mantle batted .317, but it was not high enough for team honors. The teammate who stroked the ball for a blistering .348 was

a. Elston Howard
b. Johnny Blanchard
c. Hector Lopez

267. The great heavyweight boxing champion who became his good friend was

a. Rocky Marciano
b. Floyd Patterson
c. Muhammad Ali

268. In the locker room after games, Billy Martin and Mantle enjoyed which fun activity?

a. Ping-Pong
b. poker
c. water pistol fights

269. In his book *The Quality of Courage*, Mickey honors the bravest man he ever knew, who was

a. his father
b. John F. Kennedy
c. Jackie Robinson

270. The Yankee with a leading .687 slugging percentage in 1961 was

Multiple Choice

    a. Elston Howard
    b. Roger Maris
    c. Mickey Mantle

271. In Mickey's 1988 video, *An American Dream Comes to Life*, he says that the "best all-around player who ever lived" was

    a. Stan Musial
    b. Joe DiMaggio
    c. Ted Williams

272. The Detroit Tiger not pictured with Mantle and Maris on the 1964 Topps baseball card entitled "A.L. Bombers" is

    a. Norm Cash
    b. Bill Freehan
    c. Al Kaline

273. The title of the book Dick Shaap wrote about Mickey in 1961 was

    a. *Mantle of Courage*
    b. *Mickey Mantle: The Indispensable Yankee*
    c. *Switch Hitter*

274. His sixteenth World Series home run broke Babe Ruth's record. He accomplished this feat in

    a. 1961
    b. 1962
    c. 1964

275. Mantle said that his "most treasured baseball item" was a personalized ball from

    a. Babe Ruth
    b. Ty Cobb
    c. Roger Maris

276. Mantle made most of his money in the 1980s and '90s from

   a. playing golf
   b. the stock market
   c. signing autographs

277. In 1958, author Gene Schoor wrote

   a. *Mickey Mantle of the Yankees*
   b. *Courageous Yankee*
   c. *Superstar*

278. In 1961, Mickey hit 6 triples, tying

   a. Clete Boyer
   b. Bobby Richardson
   c. Tony Kubek

279. The first time Mick took the New York subway, he got off at

   a. The Polo Grounds
   b. Madison Square Garden
   c. Ebbets Field

280. In the 1950s, this Washington Senators pitcher always claimed to be a faster runner than Mickey. He was

   a. Camilio Pascual
   b. Pedro Ramos
   c. Jim Hannah

Multiple Choice

281. Throughout the 1980s and '90s, Mickey was the top draw in

  a. public speaking
  b. sports cards and memorabilia
  c. country-western concerts

282. The Yankee who led the 1961 team in stolen bases with 12 was

  a. Bobby Richardson
  b. Mickey Mantle
  c. Clete Boyer

283. Mickey saw only one play on Broadway in 1956. It was

  a. *Damn Yankees*
  b. *Annie*
  c. *Jesus Christ Superstar*

284. In Mickey Mantle's restaurant, they have

  a. a poster of *Safe at Home*
  b. his first home-run ball
  c. his five-hundredth home-run ball

285. The American League manager who invented the "Mantle Shift" to defend against Mick in 1956 was

  a. George Strickland
  b. Lou Boudreau
  c. Alvin Dark

286. The only time Mickey cried after losing a professional game was after the World Series loss to

  a. Brooklyn
  b. Pittsburgh
  c. St. Louis

287. When Mantle was sent to Kansas City in the minors in 1951, his manager was

   a. George Selkirk
   b. Charlie Dressen
   c. Leo Durocher

288. Mick always seemed to hit a home run when the celebrity in attendance was

   a. Milton Berle
   b. President Eisenhower
   c. Bruce Springsteen

289. Mickey once said that "the greatest hitter I ever saw" was

   a. Ted Williams
   b. Babe Ruth
   c. Willie Mays

290. Mantle also said that "the best clutch hitter I ever saw" was

   a. Hank Aaron
   b. Yogi Berra
   c. Duke Snider

291. Mickey once said that in a big game "the only pitcher I'd want pitching for me would be"

   a. Bob Feller
   b. Sandy Koufax
   c. Whitey Ford

Multiple Choice

292. Mantle always considered the greatest catch he ever made to be the one in the World Series off the bat of

   a. Gil Hodges
   b. Orlando Cepeda
   c. Tim McCarver

293. Mickey had his first pizza with

   a. Phil Rizzuto
   b. Joe DiMaggio
   c. Bill Skowron

294. In 1956, he hit his fifty-second home run of the season off of

   a. Frank Sullivan
   b. Bob Porterfield
   c. Dick Radatz

295. Where did Mickey meet Whitey Ford for the first time?

   a. at Whitey's wedding
   b. in the minor leagues
   c. at Spring Training

296. Mick once said that "the best lefty I ever faced" was

   a. Warren Spahn
   b. Sandy Koufax
   c. Steve Carlton

297. Before going to work in the mines in the morning, Mickey used to milk how many cows?

   a. 1
   b. 9
   c. 16

298. Mickey's only World Series grand slammer came off the Brooklyn Dodgers. The pitcher who served it up was

   a. Carl Erskine
   b. Russ Meyer
   c. Don Newcombe

299. The hurler who served up Mickey's homer in Don Larsen's perfect World Series game in 1956 was

   a. Sal Maglie
   b. Sandy Koufax
   c. Clem Labine

300. He was interviewed on *The Greatest Sports Legend* video by

   a. Frank Gifford
   b. Tony Kubek
   c. Paul Hornung

301. Mickey's first memorabilia show was at

   a. Madison Square Garden
   b. the Atlantic City Convention Hall
   c. Hofstra University

Do You Remember?

In game number 7 of the 1952 World Series against the Brooklyn Dodgers, the Mick blasted a towering homer in the sixth inning off of Joe Black. The ball traveled onto Bedford Avenue. It was Mickey's second round-tripper in two days.

Multiple Choice

302. For his first show Mantle was paid

   a. $2,000
   b. $5,000
   c. $25,000

303. The Mick ran the bases with his head down after blasting a homer because

   a. he was shy
   b. he didn't want to show the pitcher up
   c. he was showing off

304. In 1971, the product he endorsed in *Life* magazine was?

   a. Kellogg's Corn Flakes
   b. Kretschmer Wheat Germ
   c. Ford Mustang

305. Mantle's height on his final baseball card was listed as

   a. 6´
   b. 6´1´´
   c. 5´9´´

306. His weight was listed as

   a. 200 pounds
   b. 197 pounds
   c. 194 pounds

307. In 1990, Mick was T-E-A-M spokesman for

   a. AIDS
   b. Multiple Sclerosis
   c. Arthritis

308. In another *Life* magazine ad, Mickey was pictured with

   a. Bart Starr
   b. Y. A. Tittle
   c. Johnny Unitas

309. His last cover picture and feature story in *Baseball Digest* was titled

   a. "The Last Superstar"
   b. "Mickey Retires"
   c. "Exit for Mantle?"

310. The first domed-stadium home run was hit by

   a. Frank Howard
   b. Roger Maris
   c. Mickey Mantle

311. Mantle shares the record for hitting safely in consecutive All-Star Games with

   a. Stan Musial
   b. Roberto Clemente
   c. Joe Morgan

312. The player who worshipped Mantle as a boy and eventually became his teammate was

   a. Steve Balboni
   b. Phil Linz
   c. Bobby Murcer

313. He lost the 1960 MVP by 3 votes and the 1961 MVP by 4 votes, both times to

   a. Roger Maris
   b. Harmon Killebrew
   c. Al Kaline

Multiple Choice

314. Mantle's last visit to Yankee Stadium was

a. Oldtimers' Day 1994
b. Memorial Day 1994
c. Labor Day 1994

315. One of Mantle's biggest regrets in baseball was

a. not hitting 61 homers
b. not finishing with a .300 career average
c. not batting exclusively righty

316. In 1994, Mickey patched up a broken relationship with

a. Lee Thomas
b. Horace Clarke
c. Jim Bouton

317. The liver Mickey received as a transplant came from a young man from

a. Nebraska
b. Idaho
c. New Jersey

318. The hospital where Mick spent his final days was

a. Parkland Memorial
b. Baylor University
c. Long Valley

319. Which of Mickey's sons played for Alexandria in the low minors in 1978?

a. David
b. Mickey Jr.
c. Danny

320. The doctor who was not one of Mickey's physicians at Baylor University Hospital was

    a. Dr. Robert Goldstein
    b. Dr. Goran Klintmalm
    c. Dr. James Bulman

321. Mantle holds the All-Star record for most

    a. home runs
    b. stolen bases
    c. strikeouts

322. Mickey holds the dubious distinction of striking out the most in World Series play. In 65 games, how many times did he whiff?

    a. 50
    b. 54
    c. 61

323. The Mick's last major league hit ruined a potential no-hitter by

    a. Jim Kaat
    b. Frank Lary
    c. Luis Tiant

324. Whose nose did Mickey break one day while throwing his outstanding knuckleball in pregame warmups?

    a. John Blanchard
    b. Elston Howard
    c. Jake Gibbs

325. The Yankees' team doctor who treated many of Mickey's injuries was

   a. Dr. Sidney Gaynor
   b. Dr. John T. O'Brien
   c. Dr. Joseph Krzyzkowski

326. The only time he batted righty against a righty pitcher was when he faced

   a. Camilio Pascual
   b. Hoyt Wilhelm
   c. Jim "Mudcat" Grant

327. In high school, he played in the Lucky 7 Conference against

   a. Doc Medich
   b. Bud Daley
   c. Ralph Terry

328. When they were in the clubhouse after games, Mickey and Billy Martin loved to listen to stories about Babe Ruth, told by the clubhouse man named

   a. Pete Sheehy
   b. Joe McCarthy
   c. Jim McCoy

329. In 1962, Mick bet sportswriter Phil Pepe that 20 home runs would be hit by which rookie?

   a. Phil Linz
   b. Joe Pepitone
   c. Tom Tresh

330. The Mickey Mantle funny song which became a hit with Yankees teammates was called

   a. "Cowtown"
   b. "Yankee Frankees"
   c. "Win, Yanks, Win"

331. Mantle's least favorite umpire was

   a. Hank Soares
   b. Ken Burkhart
   c. Bill Valentine

332. On opening day in 1956, the Mick became the first player to hit 2 home runs in one game over the center field fence at

   a. Griffith Stadium
   b. Shibe Park
   c. Comiskey Park

333. A few years ago, Mickey was interviewed on "The King of All Media's" top-rated, New York-based radio show. The show was

   a. Rush Limbaugh
   b. Howard Stern
   c. Imus

334. A member of Mickey's team of doctors at Baylor University Hospital was

   a. Dr. Joseph Stanley Jaskowiak
   b. Dr. Albert Gomolka Jr.
   c. Dr. Daniel DeMarco

335. Pictured on the cover of the August 18, 1961, issue of *Life* magazine with Mickey was

Multiple Choice

   a. Roger Maris
   b. Babe Ruth
   c. Maris and Babe Ruth

336. Mantle had his best season for hits in 1956. He collected

   a. 205
   b. 196
   c. 188

337. On his 1956 Topps baseball card, the Mick is shown

   a. stealing a base
   b. reaching into the stands to rob a homer
   c. in a batting pose

338. Back in 1949, while playing for Independence in the K-O-M League, Mickey blasted a towering homer off of

   a. Ray Stockton
   b. Don Schwall
   c. Joe Nuxhall

339. Which outstanding comedian, a close friend of Mantle's, was given a seat from the old Yankee Stadium by the Mick?

   a. Robin Williams
   b. Billy Crystal
   c. Jay Leno

340. The slugger who defeated Mickey in the popular Home-Run Derby by a 9–8 score was

   a. Eddie Matthews
   b. Al Kaline
   c. Harmon Killebrew

A muscular Mickey shown in his prime, loosening up at spring training. This never-before-published photo was taken by his friend Herb Perle of East Brunswick, NJ.

Mickey Mantle Trivia Questions

Fill in the Blank

One of the most valuable players ever to play the game, Mickey Mantle spent almost his entire career, day in, day out, with crippling injuries, but always gave 100 percent. Every big league team today has a MVP. He's the guy who always seems to get the big hit, or the pitcher who always comes through in the important showdowns. Cal Ripken, Barry Bonds, Greg Maddux, Joe Carter, Sammy Sosa, Barry Larkin, Jeff Bagwell, Ryne Sandberg, Bernie Williams, Juan Gonzalez, Frank Thomas, Ken Griffey Jr., and Todd Hundley have all been MVPs on their teams in the '90s. They would most definitely make the "Mickey Mantle Elite MVP Club."

You can become a member too, if you answer 25 of the 87 Fill in the Blanks correctly. If you correctly answer 18 to 24, you would then be the runner-up in the MVP race.

Hang in there!

Fill in the Blank

1. Mickey had _____ sisters.
2. He had _____ brothers.
3. Before his dad taught him to switch-hit, he was originally a _____.
4. Mickey was _____ _____ on the high school newspaper.
5. When he broke into the minors, Mickey played _____.
6. _____ _____ was his first Yankee manager.
7. He played _____ _____ in his first big league start.
8. As a rookie, Mick wore uniform number _____.
9. In 1951 the Mantles bought a home in Commerce with _____ rooms.
10. The Mick captured the elusive Triple Crown in _____.
11. He had his last big year when he was _____ years old.
12. Mickey blasted _____ round-trippers in 1961.
13. Knee problems forced him to learn the new position of _____ _____ in 1967.
14. _____ former teammates named their sons after Mickey.
15. Mickey played on 18 Yankees teams, and _____ made it to the World Series.

Fill in the Blank

16. Mick played in the inaugural game at _____ in 1965.

17. He hit _____ successive home runs in 1962.

18. The Mick came through with _____ extra-inning homers in his career.

19. Mantle broke _____ _____'s World Series home run mark.

20. He hit his first major league four-bagger in 19___ .

21. That first big league homer was against the _____ _____ _____.

22. _____ _____ served Mickey's one-hundredth career homer.

23. The Mick blasted _____ dingers against the Cardinals in the 1964 World Series.

24. He hit his final home run at Yankee Stadium in 1968 against the _____ _____.

25. Mickey and Merlyn had _____ children.

26. His dad started teaching him to switch-hit at age _____.

27. At age ten, he played for his first baseball team in the Pee Wee Division of a Junior League. His position was _____.

28. While at Commerce High School in the fall of 1946, he was selected to the all-district football team. His position was _____.

29. Mickey was primarily a shortstop in high school. He also played _____.

30. In his first big league game in 1951, he batted _____ in the order.

31. Career home run number 200 came against the _____ _____.

32. Mickey's dad, "Mutt," died from _____ _____.

33. _____ _____ became Mantle's second big league manager, in 1961.

34. The Mick's three-hundredth home run was hit at _____ _____.

35. In 1952, he finished _____ in the American League MVP race.

36. Mickey blasted his five-hundredth home run at _____ _____.

37. In 1957, he batted a lofty .365 and finished ____ in the American League.

38. The Mantle ethnic background was mainly _____.

39. There were _____ rooms in the house where Mickey was born.

40. Mick crunched his monumental five hundredth round-tripper against the _____ _____.

41. Mickey once did a commercial on television for _____ cereal.

42. Mickey and Merlyn went to a _____ on their first date.

43. His first military classification was _____.

44. Mick was driving a _____ automobile in 1953.

45. _____ _____ was Mickey's best friend.

Fill in the Blank

46. Mantle had _____ surgery in 1956.

47. After his retirement, he worked as a color commentator for _____.

48. He began work in 1985 for the _____ Casino in Atlantic City.

49. The Mick became the first player in history to earn _____ in a season.

50. Mickey played first base for _____ years.

51. The most homers he hit in one year was _____.

Did You Know?

At a 1995 press conference after his liver transplant, Mickey said, "Kids, don't be like me."

52. Mickey captured _____ batting championship(s).

53. The most career home runs (80) he hit against one team came against the _____.

54. In 1964, Mickey and his son _____ did an ad for *Look* and *Post* magazines.

55. Mantle won _____ RBI titles.

56. Mickey was considered a _____ type of driver.

57. On the Commerce High School basketball team, he starred at the _____ position.

58. In August 1951, his draft status was reevaluated, and he was classified _____.

59. Mick hit _____ grand slam homer(s) in World Series play.

60. In his first World Series game, he batted _____ in the order.

61. Mickey's old teammate, _____ _____ became the manager of the Yankees in 1964.

62. Mantle was turned down by the military ____ times.

63. In 1957, Mickey and his family moved from Oklahoma to _____, _____.

64. The Mantles' son _____ had Hodgkins disease.

65. Mickey went to the _____ _____ ____ for alcoholism treatment.

66. He received a _____ transplant on June 8, 1995.

67. Mantle was selected Most Valuable Player in the American League ____ times.

68. Mickey hit _____ career pinch-hit grand slammers.

69. The Mick belted three home runs in a single game _____ times in his career.

70. Mantle was touted as a possible replacement for _____ _____ in 1951.

71. Over his last two years, Mick topped the Yankees in _____ _____.

72. He signed an exclusive baseball card contract with the _____ _____ company in the 1980s.

73. In his book, *October 1964,* author David Halberstam devotes chapter _____ entirely to Mickey Mantle.

Fill in the Blank

74. Following the 1953 World Series, Merlyn and Mickey went to _____ on vacation.

75. Mickey batted _____ in the powerful 1964 Yankees lineup.

76. Mickey's playing height was listed at _____ _____ in 1961.

77. Mantle's fabled number 7 uniform was the _____ to be retired by the New York Yankees.

78. He preferred _____ movies in the 1950s.

79. The Mick always considered himself a better hitter batting _____.

80. When he retired, he was in _____ place on the all-time home-run list.

81. Mickey always loved listening to _____ music.

82. Whitey Ford and Mantle ran their Fantasy Baseball Camp _____ times per year.

83. Mickey's height was listed at _____ _____ on his 1951 Bowman rookie Baseball card.

84. He would not autograph _____ _____ at memorabilia shows.

85. _____ _____, noted restaurateur, was a good friend of Mickey's.

86. In his career, he played second base and third base _____ time(s).

87. Bob Costas won an _____ award for his obituary on Mickey Mantle on NBC Nightly News.

As you can see, the lineup for a spectacular Sports Cards and Memorabilia Show at Trump Plaza in Atlantic City in 1991 was loaded with talent. Pictured (*left to right*): Show Promoter Fred Davies, Yogi Berra (*in the black jacket*), Pee Wee Reese (*in the white jacket*), Stan Musial (*third from right*), Mickey Mantle (*second from right*), and Show Promoter Tom Catal (*right*).

Mickey Remembered

Mickey Mantle was loved and admired by people from all walks of life. His awesome talents, boyish charm, and charisma endeared him to millions. The following are quotes from well-known athletes and celebrities who were touched by Mickey Mantle:

Joe DiMaggio—
"I saw Mickey break in, and he had standout written all over him. He needed a little more experience and was sent down to our minor league club, but when he returned, everyone could see he was going to be an exceptionally fine player. We'll miss him."

Phil Rizzuto—
"Our families were exceptionally close, and our kids practically grew up together. I'm so sorry he had to suffer as he did. He left a great legacy, and he'll be loved for so many things. We all love him so much, I hate to talk about him in the past tense. Mickey always played hard and never complained. That's the way he was to the very end, never complaining—and telling jokes. He kept telling fans, 'I'm not giving up.' That was so typical of him."

Dallas Green—
"I don't think you'll see players who are injured like he was play. Everyone around the game respected him so much

for playing the game with the physical problems he had. It was a tremendous show of courage. That probably gave him a greater amount of respect than anything."

Henry Aaron—
"Mickey meant an awful lot to me. He was a tremendous athlete. People didn't understand him the way they should have. He played ten years on one leg, but more than that, he was a tremendous person."

Mel Stottlemyre—
"It's a sad day for baseball. We lost a legend, and I lost a good friend. He was as great a player as ever stepped on the field."

Don Larsen—
"I remember he used to get very mad at himself if he failed to get a hit. I'll never forget how hard he played all the time, especially the catch he made in my perfect game."

Ralph Terry—
"From where I stood, nobody could have been better. He hit it farther and ran faster."

Al Kaline—
"He was the best player I ever played against. I know the courage he had and the physical problems he had with his legs. I respected him because he was a great player who always gave 100 percent. He was the whole package: tremendous speed and tremendous power. That's a combination you don't see much of."

Steve Howe—
"Many times, we look at ourselves

and think our problems are the worst in the world. Mickey was there to remind me, 'No, it isn't.' We need it today. Unfortunately he isn't here to give that to us anymore."

Billy Crystal—
"I feel like at age forty-seven, my childhood is finally ending."

Jerry Coleman—
"I saw the home runs. I saw the speed, the greatness. But I also saw the humility. One day after hitting a home run, he came back to the bench and said to me, 'Did you see my leg shaking?' Joe DiMaggio had an imperial presence. He knew exactly who he was, what kind of impact he made. Mickey Mantle never knew how great he was, or even who he was."

President Bill Clinton—
"As a ballplayer, Mickey Mantle inspired generations of fans with his power and grit. As a man, he faced up to his responsibilities and alerted generations to come to the dangers of alcohol abuse. He will be remembered for excellence on the baseball field, and the honor and redemption he brought to the end of his life."

Tony Kubek—
"I don't know if Mickey could have been any better or not. I just like what he was, and the way he treated us, and the way he treated the game. I think that should be his legacy."

Tom Lasorda—
"I saw one of the greatest ballplayers that ever put on a baseball uniform. He was an amazing talent. He could run, hit, and hit with power. He played in pain, but he could run like the wind."

Kent Hrbek—
"We lost a hero. We'll all be there someday, everybody knows that. He was a tough guy, tough right up to the end."

Bob Lemon—
"You never knew with the Mick. You never knew how Mickey was feeling because he had always had a big smile on his face.

Buck Showalter—
"I wore number seven until I got to the Yankees, where number seven wasn't available. A big part of the whole baseball world has passed away."

George Steinbrenner—
"He transcends any game and any team. Just as Jesse Owens was to track and field, and Michael Jordan is to basketball, Mickey Mantle is to baseball."

Jim Leyritz—
"It's definitely a loss when you're talking about a Babe Ruth or a Lou Gehrig or a Mickey Mantle. That was where the words Yankee Pride and Yankee Tradition came from."

N.Y. Mayor Rudy Giuliani—
"Mickey Mantle represented something special to all of us—massive power, great talent, and youth. The image of number seven in pinstripes finishing his home-run swing will live in our memories forever. He was particularly special to all New Yorkers for his leadership of some of the greatest teams in the history of baseball—particularly the 1961 Yankees."

Bernie Williams—
"Mickey was a very special individual. It's a very sad day for all of us here."

Don Mattingly—

"We [current Yankees] understand who he was and what he did for our organization. We send our blessings to his family."

Whitey Ford—

"He is the greatest player I ever played with and one of my best friends. Mickey and I had a lot of fun. My family lost a great friend and a truly wonderful person. Now that both Mickey and Billy Martin are gone, I'll never have friends like them again."

Darryl Strawberry—

"I heard him say that if he had taken better care of himself he didn't know what he would've been capable of doing. That rubbed off on me because I wonder if I had taken better care of me what I would have done."

Yogi Berra—

"He was a leader, like DiMaggio. He always said he looked up to Joe, even though he was only with him one year. After that, Mickey took over as the leader."

Mel Allen—

"He had the attributes that no other player ever had. He will always be remembered as one of the greatest ballplayers of all time."

Bobby Murcer—

"I think the reason people loved him so much was that he portrayed the innocence of what we all want to be. I don't think that to this day Mickey realized how people felt about him, how he touched their lives, so many fans....But everybody knew Mickey Mantle and loved Mickey Mantle. He was my idol, and he still is my idol."

Ron Darling—

"He's part of Americana, part of the folklore of this country...a guy who grew up in Oklahoma and became arguably the greatest power-hitting switch-hitter ever."

Gene Woodling—

"I've never seen an athlete like the Mick. He had so much ability, far more than DiMaggio. The most remarkable thing was that home run he hit in Washington, the five-hundred-footer. A lot of players hit there like Ruth and Foxx, and they didn't come close to hitting it out. But I'll tell you what—the next night he hit one in St. Louis at the old Sportsman's Park that went farther."

Hank Bauer—

"That ball he hit in Washington was one of the longest ever. I remember he got jammed one time at Yankee Stadium, and popped the ball up. He threw his bat down on the ground, but the ball kept carrying and went into the bleachers."

Bill "Moose" Skowron—

"He hit a fly ball at Yankee Stadium one time with a broken bat. He got angry and threw his bat down on the ground, but it kept carrying and the next thing you know it was gone. He also hit two in Washington off Camilio Pascual that went between those horns in the bullpen. That was the farthest I've seen him hit one."

Jim Kaat—

"It used to be that you did not fraternize around the batting cage at all. But the first time I played against the Yankees I snuck up near the cage to see him hit. The sound of the ball off the bat was enough to make me run back to the dugout. It was intimidation."

Andy Carey—
"There was nobody who didn't love him. It was an honor to play with him."

Joe Pepitone—
"He took me in when I was a rookie. He said, 'Kid, you stay with me. You room with me.' We had a couple of beers with each other a couple of times. Sometimes our talks got pretty deep. So I know his innermost thoughts. I'll never be able to get him out of my mind."

Kyle Rote—
"They were always in the World Series, so for the first couple of games of the season, we shared the locker. He was a great locker mate. I've known him for a long time, and he's always been the same Mickey. People would come up to him, worship him, and he would get embarrassed. That was the type of guy he was."

Reggie Jackson—
"It's funny, a hero is something that is always special. Heroes are absolutely special because they give people hope. They give people somebody to look up to, they give people a dream. I think Mickey Mantle was such a plain, regular fellow, such an honest person, such a humble guy, he was the perfect hero."

Bob Costas—
"We didn't just root for him, we felt for him. He was the most compelling baseball hero of our lifetime."

Acknowledgments

First and foremost, I would like to thank my Lord, Jesus Christ, for giving me the ability to write, and most of all for showing me how to persevere and rise above the many obstacles in the road of life.

I could not have succeeded without the help of my former Kean College of New Jersey teacher, and now wonderful friend, Dr. Kenneth R. Benson. He served for many years as Kean's physical education, Health & Recreation Department chairman, and is a renowned author who has had several books published in his field of expertise. His advice, guidance, and consultations were a tremendous help.

My dear cousin, Louise Burkard Roberts, president of Paris/USA Modeling Agency in New York, was also most helpful; her tireless efforts to steer me in the right direction in the publishing arena were definitely appreciated.

I would like to thank Conrad "Dink" Cyriax Esq., for legal consultation, and a special thank you goes to my daughter Sarah Burkard Raymond and her husband Peter of East Newport, Maine. Her faith, love, and support were always given to me, regardless of any challenge I may have faced. I would also like to thank my wife Nancy and my relatives, who were always supportive. Editor Jim Ellison of Carol Publishing Group has definitely won my special Most Valuable Player Award for his tireless efforts and expertise in helping to make this book a total success. And, last but hardly least, I want to thank my close friends, who were always there to lend an ear and give me the moral support I needed at various times. Thank you all!

Mantle's official plaque at the National Baseball Hall of Fame and Museum at Cooperstown, New York

Mickey Mantle Trivia Answers

True or False Answers

1. True
2. False—Commerce, Oklahoma
3. True
4. False—Independence
5. False—truck driver in mines
6. False—Merlyn
7. True
8. True
9. False—2,500
10. False—1952
11. True
12. False—565 feet
13. True
14. False—1962
15. False—2,145
16. False—52

17. True
18. False—$1,500
19. False—130
20. True
21. True
22. True
23. True
24. False—46
25. True
26. False—Tigers
27. False—42
28. True
29. False—$75,000
30. False—43
31. True
32. True
33. False—16
34. True
35. True
36. False—1960
37. False—3 times
38. False—he hit 2 homers
39. False—Barbara
40. False

True or False Answers

41. False—372
42. True
43. True
44. False—$30,000
45. False—1 (he was injured and batted only 6 times)
46. False—1964
47. False—1,677
48. False—Charles
49. True
50. False—1985
51. True
52. True
53. False—1953
54. True
55. False—Commerce Comet
56. True
57. False—first base coach
58. True
59. False—$7,500
60. False—Danny's Hideaway
61. True
62. False—2 horses
63. False—1,734
64. True

65. False—1955
66. False—Blue Goose No. 1
67. True
68. False—$54
69. True
70. True
71. False
72. False—right field
73. False—Fort Lee
74. True
75. False—6
76. True
77. False—322
78. True
79. True
80. True
81. False—450 feet
82. True
83. False—39
84. True
85. False—*Joplin Globe*
86. True
87. True
88. False—*The Education of a Baseball Player*

True or False Answers

89. True
90. True
91. False—1961
92. False—195
93. False—$5,000
94. True
95. False—Casey Stengel
96. True
97. True
98. False—1969
99. True
100. False—7
101. False—700
102. True
103. False—1952
104. False—$20,000
105. True
106. False—$12,500
107. False—18 years
108. False—Bill "Moose" Skowron
109. True

Multiple Choice Answers

1. c	20. b	39. b	58. b
2. c	21. b	40. a	59. b
3. a	22. b	41. a	60. c
4. c	23. c	42. c	61. b
5. a	24. c	43. b	62. b
6. a	25. a	44. b	63. a
7. c	26. c	45. b	64. b
8. a	27. c	46. c	65. a
9. b	28. c	47. a	66. a
10. c	29. a	48. b	67. a
11. b	30. b	49. c	68. b
12. a	31. a	50. a	69. c
13. b	32. c	51. c	70. c
14. b	33. b	52. c	71. a
15. a	34. c	53. c	72. a
16. c	35. b	54. c	73. b
17. c	36. a	55. c	74. c
18. a	37. b	56. b	75. b
19. c	38. a	57. a	76. c

Multiple Choice Answers

77. b	101. b	125. b	149. b
78. b	102. a	126. c	150. b
79. b	103. c	127. b	151. a
80. a	104. a	128. c	152. c
81. c	105. b	129. c	153. a
82. b	106. c	130. b	154. a
83. c	107. b	131. a	155. c
84. c	108. a	132. b	156. a
85. c	109. c	133. b	157. b
86. c	110. c	134. c	158. a
87. a	111. b	135. a	159. a
88. a	112. b	136. b	160. c
89. b	113. a	137. a	161. c
90. c	114. b	138. c	162. a
91. a	115. a	139. c	163. a
92. c	116. a	140. a	164. b
93. b	117. c	141. c	165. c
94. a	118. a	142. a	166. c
95. b	119. a	143. c	167. c
96. a	120. a	144. a	168. b
97. c	121. c	145. b	169. a
98. b	122. b	146. b	170. b
99. c	123. c	147. a	171. c
100. a	124. a	148. c	172. b

173. c	197. b	221. c	245. a
174. a	198. c	222. a	246. b
175. b	199. a	223. c	247. c
176. b	200. b	224. b	248. a
177. c	201. a	225. a	249. b
178. b	202. b	226. c	250. c
179. a	203. a	227. a	251. a
180. c	204. c	228. c	252. a
181. b	205. c	229. a	253. a
182. c	206. c	230. c	254. c
183. c	207. b	231. a	255. c
184. a	208. b	232. c	256. b
185. b	209. a	233. b	257. b
186. b	210. a	234. a	258. b
187. b	211. c	235. c	259. b
188. a	212. c	236. a	260. c
189. b	213. b	237. a	261. a
190. a	214. a	238. b	262. b
191. a	215. b	239. b	263. a
192. a	216. c	240. b	264. c
193. c	217. a	241. a	265. a
194. c	218. a	242. b	266. a
195. c	219. c	243. b	267. a
196. a	220. c	244. c	268. c

Multiple Choice Answers

269. a	293. c	317. c
270. c	294. b	318. b
271. b	295. a	319. b
272. b	296. b	320. c
273. b	297. c	321. c
274. c	298. b	322. b
275. c	299. a	323. c
276. c	300. c	324. c
277. a	301. c	325. a
278. c	302. a	326. b
279. a	303. b	327. c
280. b	304. b	328. a
281. b	305. a	329. c
282. b	306. c	330. a
283. a	307. c	331. c
284. a	308. c	332. a
285. b	309. c	333. b
286. b	310. c	334. c
287. a	311. c	335. c
288. b	312. c	336. c
289. a	313. a	337. b
290. b	314. a	338. a
291. c	315. b	339. b
292. a	316. c	340. c

Fill in the Blank Answers

1. 1
2. 3
3. righty
4. sports editor
5. shortstop
6. Casey Stengel
7. right field
8. number 6
9. 7
10. 1956
11. 32
12. 54
13. first base
14. 6
15. 12
16. The Astrodome
17. 4
18. 14
19. Babe Ruth
20. 1951
21. Chicago White Sox
22. Chicago White Sox
23. 3
24. Boston Red Sox
25. 4
26. five
27. catcher
28. halfback
29. pitcher
30. third
31. Detroit Tigers
32. Hodgkins disease
33. Ralph Houk
34. Griffith Stadium
35. third
36. Yankee Stadium
37. second
38. English

Fill in the Blank Answers

39. two
40. Baltimore Orioles
41. Mapo
42. movie
43. 4-F
44. Lincoln
45. Harold Youngman
46. tonsillectomy
47. ABC
48. Claridge
49. $100,000
50. 2
51. 54
52. 1
53. Washington Senators
54. Mickey Jr.
55. 1
56. slow
57. guard
58. 4-F
59. 1
60. first
61. Yogi Berra
62. 4
63. Dallas, Texas
64. Billy
65. Betty Ford Center
66. liver
67. 3
68. 1
69. 1
70. Phil Rizzuto
71. home runs
72. Upper Deck
73. 7
74. Cuba
75. fourth
76. 5´11˝
77. fourth
78. Western
79. righty
80. third
81. country
82. 3
83. 5´10˝
84. baseball bats
85. Toots Shor's
86. 1 time each
87. Emmy

Credits

Archive Photos, pp. ii, 2, 12
Ed English and Andy Hulsart, p. 32
Herb Perle, p. 80
Fred Davies, p. 88
Thank you all very much for your wonderful contributions to *The Ultimate Mickey Mantle Trivia Book.*